Rook**i**e
Read-About®
Science

The Stars

by Cody Crane

Content Consultant

Kevin Manning

Astronomer

Reading Consultant

Jeanne M. Clidas, Ph.D.

Reading Specialist

Children's Press®

An Imprint of Scholastic Inc.

Library of Congress Cataloging-in-Publication Data
Names: Crane, Cody, author.
Title: The stars/by Cody Crane.
Description: New York, NY: Children's Press, An Imprint of Scholastic Inc.,
[2018] | Series: Rookie read-about science | Includes index.
Identifiers: LCCN 2017028043 | ISBN 9780531230862 (library binding) | ISBN 9780531229811 (pbk.)
Subjects: LCSH: Stars—Juvenile literature.
Classification: LCC QB801.7 .C73 2018 | DDC 523.8—dc23
LC record available at https://lccn.loc.gov/2017028043

No part of this publication may be reproduced in whole or in part, or stored in a retrieval system, or transmitted in any form or by any means, electronic, mechanical, photocopying, recording, or otherwise, without written permission of the publisher. For information regarding permission, write to Scholastic Inc., Attention: Permissions Department, 557 Broadway, New York, NY 10012.

Produced by Spooky Cheetah Press
Art direction: Tom Carling, Carling Design Inc.
Creative direction: Judith Christ-Lafond for Scholastic

© 2018 by Scholastic Inc. All rights reserved.

Published in 2018 by Children's Press, an imprint of Scholastic Inc.

Printed in Heshan, China 62

SCHOLASTIC, CHILDREN'S PRESS, ROOKIE READ-ABOUT®, and associated logos are trademarks and/or registered trademarks of Scholastic Inc.

4 5 6 7 8 9 10 R 27 26 25 24 23 22 21 20 19 18

Photos ©: cover main: Ian McKinnell/Getty Images; cover background: Kozachenko Maksym/Shutterstock; back cover: Per Andre Hoffmann/Getty Images; cartoon dog throughout: Kelly Kennedy; 1: Pete_LD/Getty Images; 2-3: Per Andre Hoffmann/Getty Images; 4-5: Feng Wei Photography/Getty Images; 6: M. Kulyk/Science Source; 8-9: Magictorch; 10-11: Mark Garlick/Science Source; 13: JPL-Caltech/STScI/NASA; 14: NASA; 16-17 stars: shooarts/Shutterstock; 16-17 colors: Designua/Shutterstock; 18: QAI Publishing/UIG/Getty Images; 20-21: Richard Kail/Science Source; 22 background, 23: David Trood/Getty Images; 22 inset: Ultima_Gaina/iStockphoto; 25 top: Jerry Lodriguss/Science Source; 25 bottom: Constantin Opris/Dreamstime; 26: MSFC/NASA; 27 top: Robert Llewellyn/Getty Images; 28-29 graph paper: Natbasil/Dreamstime; 28-29 paper clips: Angela Jones/Dreamstime; 28 background: Steven Puetzer/Getty Images; 29 top: MsMoloko/iStockphoto; 30 background: Giraphics/Dreamstime; 30 right: Project with vigour/Media Bakery; 30 left: Mark Garlick/Science Source; 31 top: Sarunyu_foto/Shutterstock; 31 center top: peepo/iStockphoto; 31 bottom: Magictorch; 31 center bottom: JPL-Caltech/STScI/NASA; 32: ESA, J. Hester (ASU) and M. Weisskopf (NASA/MSFC)/NASA.

Scholastic Inc., 557 Broadway, New York, NY 10012

Table of Contents

Let's Explore the Stars!

On a clear night, twinkling stars light up the sky. Those stars are actually burning balls of gas. And they are really, really BIG! Stars only look small because they are very far away. We can see thousands of stars from our planet. But there are billions and billions of stars in space.

The stars we can see from Earth are part of the Milky Way galaxy.

I am Rocket. Do you want to explore the universe with me? Then get ready to blast off. Next stop, the stars!

The Inner Workings of a Star

Here's what goes on inside a star.

The core is superhot and dense.

Energy flows out toward the surface.

A star is hottest at its center. It can reach millions of degrees. PHEW!

1

Fire in the Sky

Stars are mostly made up of two types of gases: hydrogen (**high**-druh-juhn) and helium (**hee**-lee-uhm). A star is so big that a huge weight presses down on its center. The hydrogen gets tightly squeezed. That forces some of the gas to combine and turn into helium. The change produces **energy**—a lot of it. Stars give off this energy as heat and light.

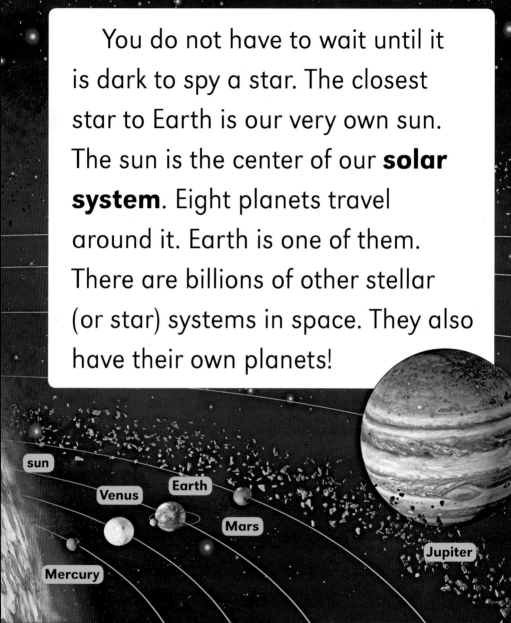

You do not have to wait until it is dark to spy a star. The closest star to Earth is our very own sun. The sun is the center of our **solar system**. Eight planets travel around it. Earth is one of them. There are billions of other stellar (or star) systems in space. They also have their own planets!

sun

Venus

Earth

Mars

Jupiter

Mercury

The second-closest star to Earth is Proxima Centauri (**prok**-suh-muh sen-**tawr**-ee). It is about 260,000 times as far away as our sun!

Neptune

Uranus

Saturn

The sun provides heat and light to our solar system.

From Earth, the Milky Way looks like a faint band of light that stretches across the sky.

In space, billions of stars cluster together to form galaxies. Our sun and the stars we see from Earth are part of the Milky Way galaxy. The Milky Way is shaped like a giant pinwheel. A galaxy can also be shaped like a ball. Some galaxies do not have a specific shape. They just look like blobs of stars.

There are trillions of galaxies in space. Each is filled with billions of stars!

2

A Star's Life

Space is filled with huge clouds of gas and dust called **nebulas**. That is where stars are born. Stars take millions of years to form. First, **gravity** pulls bits of gas and dust together into a ball. The ball grows bigger and bigger. It starts to spin and heat up. Finally, the ball bursts to life. A star is born!

The word "nebula" means "cloud."

This is the Orion nebula.

Stars Size Comparison

A star's size depends on its type.

red dwarf

blue-white giant

yellow dwarf (our sun)

red supergiant

Stars gather different amounts of dust and gas as they form. So some are bigger than others. Scientists call the smallest stars dwarfs. They can be the size of Earth. Larger stars are known as giants. Even bigger stars are called supergiants. They can be more than 1,000 times as large as our sun. How brightly a star shines depends on its size and how hot it is.

Do you want to know why these stars have different color names? Turn to the next page!

Scientists know how hot a star is because of its color. The coolest stars appear red. Next come orange, yellow, and then white stars. The hottest stars glow blue.

Star Color and Temperature

Most people think of the color red as hot and blue as cool. It is the exact opposite for stars!

| 3,000°K | 4,000°K | 6,000°K | 7,000°K |

Our sun is a yellow dwarf. It is a medium temperature and size. The most common type of star is a red dwarf. Red dwarfs are relatively small and dim.

10,000°K   **20,000°K**   **30,000°K**

The outer layers of a dying star drift away.

When a Star Dies

Every star grows old and dies.
That happens as it slowly uses up its
hydrogen fuel. For example, our sun
will expand as it nears the end of its
life. It will grow
into a giant. Its
outer layers will
drift away. A white
dwarf will be left behind.
The white dwarf will grow
cold and dark over time.

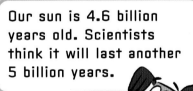

Our sun is 4.6 billion years old. Scientists think it will last another 5 billion years.

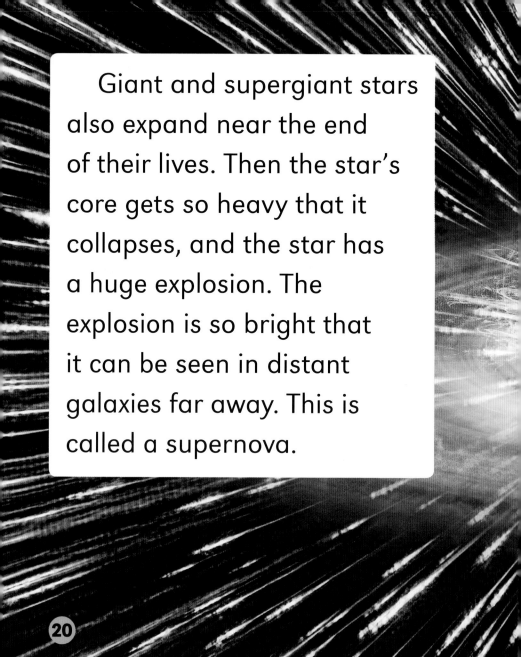

Giant and supergiant stars also expand near the end of their lives. Then the star's core gets so heavy that it collapses, and the star has a huge explosion. The explosion is so bright that it can be seen in distant galaxies far away. This is called a supernova.

Our sun is not big enough to ever explode in a supernova.

The brightness of a supernova can take months to fade.

New York City's bright lights make it hard to see stars.

Hundreds of years ago, there was no electricity. Thousands of stars could be seen in the night sky.

Looking Up

How many stars you can see at night depends on where you are. It can be hard to see stars in a city. Street lamps and buildings create too much light. But you can still see thousands of twinkling stars if you travel far from cities.

People can see thousands of stars in the countryside.

Long ago, people looked for patterns in groups of stars. Pictures formed if they connected the stars with imaginary lines. These shapes are called constellations (kon-stuh-**lay**-shuhns). People named them after heroes, gods, animals, and everyday objects. For example, Leo is shaped like a lion.

There are 88 official constellations in the sky.

Little Dipper

Big Dipper

The Big and Little Dippers are familiar patterns in the sky.

The Hubble Space Telescope takes photos of distant stars and galaxies as it orbits Earth.

Hubble Space Telescope

Scientists use telescopes to study the stars. Some telescopes spy stars from Earth. Other telescopes soar

Ground telescopes let scientists look at the stars from Earth.

through space. They help scientists learn more about how stars live and die. Telescopes can even spot distant galaxies. Maybe someday we will visit stars far beyond our own!

Good night! I'm going to dream about the stars.

Observe the Stars

See which constellations you can
find in the night sky.
Be sure to ask an adult for help!

YOU WILL NEED:

- ✓ Constellation photos
- ✓ Clear night
- ✓ Small flashlight
- ✓ Mat to lie on

STEP-BY-STEP:

1 On a clear night, take a walk outside with a trusted adult. Find a spot where a lot of stars are visible. Lie down on your mat.

2 Use your flashlight to consult the constellation photos below. Which constellations do you see in the sky?

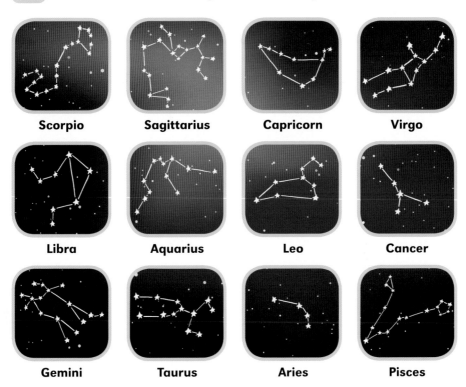

Scorpio Sagittarius Capricorn Virgo

Libra Aquarius Leo Cancer

Gemini Taurus Aries Pisces

3 Make observations on different evenings throughout the month. Does what you see change?

Think About It:
Earth moves around the sun. How might that motion affect the constellations we see throughout the year?

Stories About the Stars

Long ago, people did not know what the stars were. They made up stories about these glittering lights in the sky.

⭐ Some Native Americans believed the Milky Way was a road the dead followed to reach the afterlife.

The Ancient Greeks believed one constellation represented Orion. In Greek myths, Orion was a great hunter who carried a club.

Glossary

energy (**en**-ur-jee): power in forms such as heat, light, and motion

gravity (**grav**-ih-tee): force that pulls things toward each other; there is very little gravity in space

nebulas (**neb**-yuh-luhz): glowing clouds of gas and dust that can be seen in the night sky

solar system (**soh**-lur **siss**-tuhm): the sun and all the objects that travel around it

Index

Facts for Now

Visit this Scholastic Web site for more information
on the stars:

www.factsfornow.scholastic.com

Enter the keyword Stars

About the Author

Cody Crane is an award-winning nonfiction children's writer.
From a young age, she was set on becoming a scientist. She later
discovered that writing about science could be just as fun as the
real thing. She lives in Houston, Texas, with her husband and son.